Children of the World
Nigeria

For a free color catalog describing Gareth Stevens' list of high-quality books, call 1-800-341-3569 (USA) or 1-800-461-9120 (Canada).

For their help in the preparation of *Children of the World: Nigeria,* the writers and editor gratefully thank Mrs. Frances Hall, St. Saviour's School, Lagos, Nigeria; Dene Barton, Harare Sheraton, Zimbabwe; Cordelia C. Agboti, Lagos Sheraton, Nigeria; Philip Hall, Nigerian Conservation Foundation; Julian Ozanne, Financial Times, Nairobi, Kenya; and Romanus Nwaru of Marquette University, Milwaukee, Wisconsin.

Flag illustration on page 48, © Flag Research Center.

Library of Congress Cataloging-in-Publication Data

Lauré, Jason.
    Nigeria / by Jason Lauré and Ettagale Blauer.
       p. cm. -- (Children of the world)
    Includes index.
    Summary: Presents the life of a ten-year-old girl and her family in Nigeria, describing her home and recreational activities and discussing the people and culture of her country.
    ISBN 0-8368-0258-6
    1. Nigeria--Social life and customs--Juvenile literature. 2. Children--Nigeria--Juvenile literature. [1. Nigeria--Social life and customs. 2. Family life--Nigeria.] I. Blauer, Ettagale. II. Title. III. Series: Children of the world (Milwaukee, Wis.)
DT515.22.L48   1992
966.9--dc20   89-43199

Edited, designed, and produced by
Gareth Stevens Publishing
1555 North RiverCenter Drive, Suite 201
Milwaukee, Wisconsin 53212, USA

Series editor: Valerie Weber
Research editor: Chandrika Kaul, Ph.D.
Designer: Sharone Burris
Map design: Sheri Gibbs
Captions: Marisia Lauré

Printed in the United States of America

1 2 3 4 5 6 7 8 9 98 97 96 95 94 93 92

Children of the World
Nigeria

Text by Ettagale Blauer
Photographs by Jason Lauré

Gareth Stevens Publishing
MILWAUKEE

. . . a note about *Children of the World*:

The children of the world live in fishing towns, Arctic regions, and urban centers, on islands and in mountain valleys, on sheep ranches and fruit farms. This series follows one child in each country through the pattern of his or her life. Candid photographs show the children with their families, at school, at play, and in their communities. The text describes the dreams of the children and, often through their own words, tells how they see themselves and their lives.

Each book also explores events that are unique to the country in which the child lives, including festivals, religious ceremonies, and national holidays. The *Children of the World* series does more than tell about foreign countries. It introduces the children of each country and shows readers what it is like to be a child in that country.

Children of the World includes the following published and to-be-published titles:

Afghanistan	El Salvador	Jordan	Saudi Arabia
Argentina	England	Kenya	Singapore
Australia	Finland	Malaysia	South Africa
Austria	France	Mexico	South Korea
Belize	Greece	Morocco	Spain
Bhutan	Guatemala	Nepal	Sweden
Bolivia	Honduras	New Zealand	Tanzania
Brazil	Hong Kong	Nicaragua	Thailand
Burma (Myanmar)	Hungary	Nigeria	Turkey
Canada	India	Norway	USSR
China	Indonesia	Panama	Vietnam
Costa Rica	Ireland	Peru	West Germany
Cuba	Israel	Philippines	Yugoslavia
Czechoslovakia	Italy	Poland	Zambia
Denmark	Jamaica	Portugal	
Egypt	Japan	Romania	

. . . and about *Nigeria*:

Ten-year-old Nike Olakunri is a child of the Yoruba tribe, one of the largest ethnic groups in Nigeria. Fascinated by her country's cultural diversity, Nike goes to an "All Nigerian Food and Music Festival" to see the varied menus and musical tastes of other parts of Nigeria. She also attends a multi-cultural private school in Lagos and speaks both Yoruba and English fluently.

To enhance this book's value in libraries and classrooms, comprehensive reference sections include up-to-date information about Nigeria's geography, demographics, languages, currency, education, cultures, industry, and natural resources. *Nigeria* also features a bibliography, glossaries, activities and research projects, and discussions of such subjects as Lagos, the country's history, languages, political system, and ethnic and religious composition.

The living conditions and experiences of children in Nigeria vary according to economic, environmental, and ethnic circumstances. The reference sections help bring to life for young readers the diversity and richness of the culture and heritage of Nigeria. Of particular interest are discussions of the changes in government, the various tribes, languages, and cultures, and the role of Nigeria as a potential leader in Africa.

CONTENTS

LIVING IN NIGERIA:
Nike, a Yoruba Girl

Nike Olakunri is a ten-year-old girl from Nigeria, a country on the west coast of Africa. Nike (pronounced NEE-kee) lives in Ikoyi, one of the sections of Lagos, the nation's biggest city.

Nike's family is Yoruba, one of the largest ethnic groups in Nigeria. These people have an ancient tradition in Nigeria and have been traced back more than 1,000 years. Nike's first name, the one her grandparents gave her, is Olanike (pronounced oh-lan-NEE-kee), but she's usually called Nike, which is her nickname. In the Yoruba culture, names have specific meanings that have to do with the person's birth. Olanike means "honor the person who has arrived."

Nike lives with her mother and father. She has one brother and three sisters, but all of them are much older than she. Although none of them still live at home, they often come to visit. Her grandmother lives right across the street, and Nike sees her almost every day.

Nike enjoys a moment alone with her father at their home. ▶

Nike and her mother stand in their front garden, enveloped in plants.

In Nigeria as in much of Africa, women often carry things on their heads.

At Home with Nike

Nike's family is typical of the educated class in Nigeria. Her mother is an accountant, and her father is a businessman. Her parents often come home during the day and spend time with her.

Nike lives in a sturdy house made of cinder blocks that are plastered over and painted white. Many people in the city have houses like this one, but in the countryside, most people live in much smaller wooden houses. Nike has her own room, where she studies and sleeps and where her friends come to play.

A lovely garden surrounds Nike's house with greenery. A generator in the backyard provides electricity when the power supplied by the city fails. This happens very often in Nigeria. The services and sanitary facilities provided by the city are extremely poor for a country that is wealthy in comparison to other African countries. In many neighborhoods, the sewer systems are very bad, and a foul smell often drifts through the air.

Nike spends some time in her backyard with children from the neighborhood.

Recently, on Nike's tenth birthday, her room was changed. Because it marks the first double-digit year in a person's life, ten is a very important age in Nigeria. Now she will have a much more grown-up room than she had before.

Her room is small, with a bed, two chairs, a shelf for her books, and a big picture of Nike with her niece and one of her friends. A lamp in the shape of a goose stands on the shelf beneath her windows. Nike sometimes watches the same shows North American kids see, especially "The Cosby Show" and "A Different World," on her own television set placed in a cabinet.

When Nike's friends come over to her house, they all gather in her room to play. She especially enjoys board games. Sometimes she plays with her ten-year-old niece Eloho and her eight-year-old nephew Natife, the children of her eldest sister. When Nike is alone and has finished her homework, she likes to read mystery books.

Natife teases Nike and begs for her allowance, which Nike has just stored in her hip pack.

Nike playfully hugs her goose-shaped lamp; it's really useful when she studies.

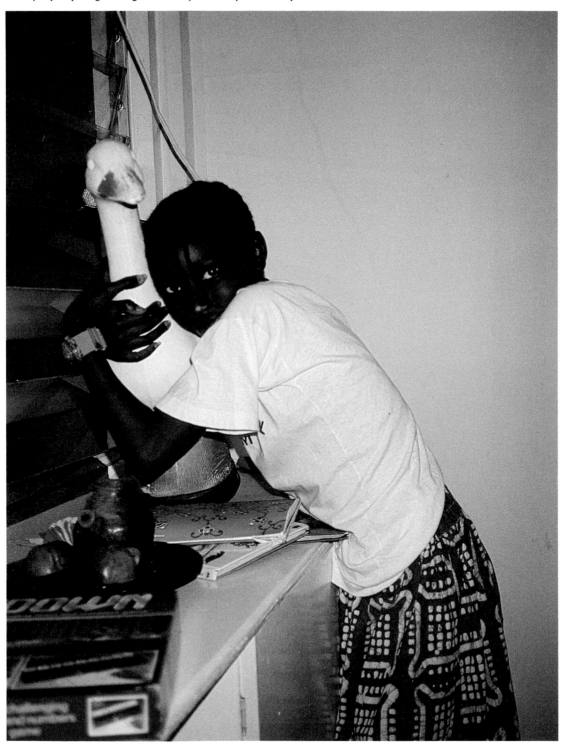

From this view of the city of Lagos at a distance, it's easy to see the contrast between the modern skyline and the shacks where many people live.

Nike Goes to School

Nike gets up at about 7:00 a.m. to get ready for school. She wears the school uniform, a T-shirt with the words "St. Saviour's School" on it and a blue tie-dyed skirt. All she has for breakfast is a cup of tea, but during the morning break at school, at 10:30 a.m., she devours a sandwich and a drink.

Nike attends school from 8:30 a.m. until 1:00 p.m. She gets a ride to school because her parents don't want her to use the local buses. They are very crowded and rather dangerous.

Nike joins her classmates in front of a school mosaic portraying the dove of peace. Each girl wears a blue and white skirt in a different pattern.

Nike lives just a mile from the military barracks where the president of Nigeria stays. Many soldiers also live there. One day, the soldiers were shooting their guns in the street because they were angry with the president and wanted to throw him out of office. Incidents like this and other threats of violence are another reason why Nike's parents don't let her go to school on her own.

Schoolmates' drawings of cars and trucks crowd the wall behind Nike.

The girls work on their lessons.

Nike's teacher, Mrs. Edet, leads the class in working out a math problem on the chalkboard.

St. Saviour's is a private school about a 15-minute drive from Nike's home. There, she has a chance to be with different kinds of children. Some, like Nike, are black Nigerians, and some are white children whose parents are from Europe. Right now, all of the teachers in the school happen to be African or European women. Nike's teacher for fifth grade is Mrs. Ema Edet.

Most children in Nigeria attend free public primary schools that teach the basics of reading and arithmetic. After primary school, they must pass a special test in order to continue their education, and their parents must pay their school fees and buy them uniforms. This is too expensive for most families — only about one-quarter of the students continue after the sixth grade.

All of Nike's classes are conducted in English, which she speaks perfectly. She also speaks Yoruba. When most Nigerian children first enter school, they are taught in their own language, often referred to as their "mother tongue." After the third grade, all students are taught in English, which is the language used to conduct business and run the government in Nigeria.

Schoolbags are hung on pegs outside the classroom.

Top: The girls share secrets as they stroll near the lagoon outside the school.
Bottom: A quiet moment during the break from classes.

18

Nike and two classmates intently play the Nigerian national anthem on their recorders.

Recess and Recorders

During recess at St. Saviour's School, the children play in the yard alongside the lagoon. It's a chance to get away from their intense studies for a brief time and enjoy the clean air coming off the water. This is a particularly lovely site in Lagos, away from the noise of the traffic and the congestion in the streets. Here, the children can really feel free to go about their play and studies.

Nike is learning to play classical Western music on her recorder at school. When she listens to music at home, she enjoys all different types, including rap songs. Two of her favorite singers are Vanilla Ice and Hammer. North American music is heard all over Africa.

Nike's Study Classes

When Nike leaves St. Saviour's School at one o'clock, she has a snack in the car because she is hurrying to the second part of her studies. Four afternoons a week, she takes private classes from 1:00 to 3:00 p.m. to practice math exercises and improve her English, especially her speed and accuracy in reading. And on some days, she has another special class from 3:00 to 4:30 p.m. in general subjects. This may seem like a lot of lessons for a ten-year-old, but Nike is a good student and really enjoys learning.

All these private classes help her prepare for a big test, called the Common Entrance Exam, that is given to all students who want to enter high school, which begins after sixth grade. Since the test is graded by a computer, Nike will have to fill out special computer cards by shading them in correctly when she answers the questions.

A pile of schoolbags under a tree is a sure sign that the students have rushed in to start their extra lessons.

The girls sit at long tables and concentrate on their answers.

Finances and Friends

Nike receives an allowance of ten *naira* a week. That's about one dollar in US money. She can buy an ice cream cone for one naira.

Street vendors are everywhere you go in Lagos, whether you are walking or in a car. The traffic is so bad here that street vending has become a kind of industry.

One day, Nike wants to buy an ice cream but doesn't have enough money. She always buys from the same ice cream vendor, so she asks, "Since I'm a regular customer, can I pay you tomorrow?" The ice cream man says yes! So she buys her ice cream on credit, with the promise to pay for it tomorrow.

Sometimes, she'll even buy a cone for Eloho and Natife. Since Nike doesn't have a brother or sister close to her own age, she enjoys having her niece and nephew to play with. They are really more like a brother and sister to her — she doesn't think of herself as being their aunt.

Nike peeks into the ice cream vendor's cart before she picks a flavor.

Nike carefully chooses some gum from a street vendor's supply. ▶

Nike Goes to a Wedding

Today, Nike's cousin Tosin is to be married at the Lagos Lawn Tennis Club. It's traditional for the bride and groom to have separate parties to celebrate the wedding. Nike goes to the bride's party dressed in a very festive Yoruba outfit that was made just for the wedding.

Many of the women at the wedding wear clothes that are distinctive to their tribe. Even different kinds of fabric are chosen by different tribes. Before the wedding, the members of the bride's and groom's families confer with one another and decide what colors they are going to wear to the wedding party. The wedding invitation not only gives the date and place of the ceremony but also notes the colors that are suggested for everyone attending.

Nike's mother was responsible for organizing the dresses for all the women in her family. She bought the fabric and sent it to her relatives so they could have dresses made for the occasion. Nike's dress is also made from this fabric.

Nike and her mother enjoy a special moment together at her cousin's wedding party.

24

The bride (right) beams as the guests crowd around to congratulate her and give her gifts.

The guests come to the wedding party to praise the groom and bride and wish them well in their married life. They give the new couple a good start in life by showering them with gifts of money; the Nigerians call this "spraying" them with money. The guests get fresh, crisp bills at the bank and then fan them out right in front of the bride, actually sticking the bills onto the bride's forehead while everyone is dancing. Then the bills are gathered up in a basket carried around by the bride's friend. Since Nigerian weddings are very expensive, this is a way of paying back the family for part of the great expense they've incurred.

Many Nigerians don't mind showing how much money something has cost. This is why they like to give money as a present instead of buying something.

Nike's mother and father know so many people, they go to a wedding almost every week of the year. These happy occasions help friends and relatives form closer relationships.

The Clothes Nigerians Wear

Although she wears a uniform for school and Western-style clothes for her everyday activities, when Nike gets dressed up for a special occasion, she wears traditional Nigerian dress. Both of her parents often wear traditional clothing. Traditional Nigerian garments are loose fitting and easy to wear. Much cooler than most Western garments, they're more comfortable during the hot and humid days because they allow air to flow through to the body.

When it's hot and sticky, Nike loves her cool coverall shorts outfit.

Above: These children from the Hausa tribe in the north wear brightly printed fabrics tied in a variety of ways to form skirts and tops. Some fabric tied around her back allows this girl to carry a younger child.

Below: Hausa men wear long, loose-fitting garments that help keep them cool. In the north, which borders the Sahara, the climate and terrain are suitable for camels, which are used to carry goods.

A woman helps her friend wrap her headdress. Women who dress in traditional clothing always wear turbans.

This Hausa woman wears a loosely tied head scarf and a long dress, both offering some protection from the fierce rays of the sun.

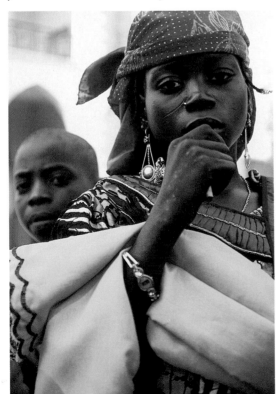

In some parts of Africa, when people become more educated, they often turn their back on traditional clothing. But this is not true in Nigeria. Most Nigerians don't try to imitate Western culture. They like to wear their traditional garments because they are so proud of them.

Nigerian women wear brightly printed fabrics for their two-piece outfits, always adding a hair tie or headdress of a matching or contrasting fabric. These are tied in distinctive and individual ways.

Children in northern Nigeria wear brightly patterned dresses and headdresses.

At a special Muslim festival, men are dressed in turbans and traditional two-layer garments.

29

The Meridien Hotel faces Bar Beach, where a woman walks, carrying dishes in a dishpan on her head.

Visiting Shola's House

Nike often goes to her friend Shola Ashaya's house to visit and go to the beach. The two girls are friends and schoolmates at St. Saviour's. Shola lives near Bar Beach on Victoria Island, one of the other main parts of Lagos that directly faces the Atlantic Ocean. Very few people go swimming here because there is a strong undertow, but people enjoy walking along the beach.

The beach is a perfect setting for religious services. From the 15th century until the early 19th century, hundreds of thousands of people were taken away from Nigeria and sold as slaves in Brazil. Generations later, when the slaves were freed, some returned to Nigeria to live. They considered Nigeria their home, and they brought their religious practices from South America, including the Santeria religion, with them. Santeria is a complicated mix of rituals, many revolving around cures. It always includes dancing as a form of worship. Here on the beach front, Santeria believers have the space to express their beliefs.

Men walk along the beach on their way to a religious service.

These people create their own church on the beach by putting up a simple structure and a cross for their religious service.

Nike and her friends learn how to braid hair by practicing on each other.

Sometimes when the girls get together at Shola's house, they braid each other's hair into corn rows, a popular hairstyle that started in Africa and then found its way to North America. It takes a long time to make the tiny braids, but the girls enjoy doing it. They talk and watch television at the same time. One of Nike's other friends, Funke Shorekan, joins in the fun.

Intricately braided hairdos have always been popular in Nigeria. After the hair is braided, it is sometimes arranged in open framework patterns. These give added height to the wearer and make her look very elegant. Braided hairdos are worn primarily by young, unmarried women.

◀ Nike concentrates on braiding Shola's hair.

Nike relaxes on the couch while she enjoys a dish of rice and stew. Ingredients used in preparing the stew include meat or fish, crayfish, tomatoes, onions, pepper, and different spices.

Popular Nigerian foods include (from left to right) *pito* beer, *epa* or peanuts, and *fura da nono* made from ground beans.

PITO BEER

Epa

Fura Da nono

The Food Nike Eats

At a festival, this woman easily balances a basket of vegetables on her head, a traditional way of carrying things.

Nike eats Western food as well as traditional Yoruba dishes. She already knows how to cook a number of traditional foods, but the thing she most likes to make for herself is popcorn, called *guguru* in Yoruba. One of her other favorite snacks is *dodo,* which are plantain chips.

Although she eats certain foods with a fork, some traditional Nigerian foods are eaten with the fingers. Nike rolls up a kind of thick porridge made of cassava flour called *eba* and dips it into an okra stew, then neatly eats it with her fingers without spilling a drop.

Like many Nigerian dishes, this dish of eba with okra soup is very spicy — which is the way most Nigerians like their food. In addition to soup stock, water, okra, and pepper, this soup contains mashed *iru,* a vegetable seasoning made from locust bean seeds; *akaun,* which is rock salt that is used to thicken the soup; and ground crayfish, a special spice.

Nike and her niece Eloho spend the day at the festival.

A Food and Music Festival

Nigeria is divided into three regions — the north, southeast, and southwest. The people in these regions each developed from completely different cultures. Throughout Nigeria, an incredible assortment of languages — at least 250 of them — are spoken. The three principal languages are Ibo, Yoruba, and Hausa. Nigerians are proud of their diverse cultures.

To celebrate all the different kinds of music and food of the nation, the "All Nigerian Food and Music Festival" is being held in Tafawa Balewa Square, which is not far from where Nike lives. This festival gives her a chance to see some of these other cultures.

Nigerians have come from all over to cook their regional dishes and to introduce these different flavors to the children of Lagos. School groups have come to the festival to learn how the dishes were made and to sample some of the foods. The names of the foods appear on labels so everyone knows exactly what they are looking at. Home economics students busily copy some recipes for the more than 60 different dishes on display.

Schoolchildren in uniforms come to learn about the foods from distinct parts of their country.

While the food is displayed, musicians from all over the country introduce the audience to music from different regions. The musicians are dressed in their regional outfits, providing a glimpse of the variety of dress and physical features among the different peoples in the many areas of Nigeria.

Nigerian music is quite well known outside of the country, both in other parts of Africa and in the United States and Canada. It's a lively music, full of spirit, and the sound makes you want to dance. One of the best known performers is King Sunny Adé. One of his bands played at the wedding of Nike's cousin.

Besides the musicians, a *griot*, an African storyteller, performs for the audience. As he spins his tale, dancers circle around him, listening and reflecting his words. In Nigeria, storytellers often lead any important occasion. For example, at a wedding, the storyteller will announce the presence of honored visitors to onlookers.

The griot begins to tell a story.

People bring special gifts to honor the griot.

Musicians from the northern state of Kano wear special festival headdresses decorated with coins.

The Culture of Kano

Nike is interested in learning everything about her country, including the north of Nigeria. The Islamic north has a rich and lively culture that is celebrated at the Durbar Festival in Kano. In the past, there were wars between the peoples of the north. When the war was over, the victorious group would stage a festival in celebration. The victorious emir would display the strength of his army through its superior horsemanship.

Now, the Durbar Festival is held when a new emir is installed or to celebrate the visit of an important person. Usually, the person has made a historic achievement or holds very high office. Foreigners are often honored with a formal reception, called a *durbar*, when they come to Nigeria. The durbar is one of the most exciting events connected with the Islamic religion.

The sultan of the state of Katsina (left) and the governor of Katsina (right) watch a parade.

The clothing styles in the hot, northern part of Nigeria are simple and cool.

Horses are crucial to the northern cultures and are richly decorated for festivals. ▶

Men in the north often cover their faces, partly because of tradition, but also as a protection from the dust and sun.

Today, as in the past, the festival's emphasis is on equestrian skill. The horses are decorated to match the clothing of their riders. Suddenly, the men start to ride at full speed toward the people watching. The dust clouds up behind them as they race forward. At the last second, just before they run into the crowd, the riders signal the horses to stop. Everyone cheers at the skill of the horsemen — and of the horses.

Here in the north, Islam plays a major role in the people's lives. Those who follow this religion are called Muslims. In many ways, Islam is more important than the government, which always seems to be changing. Islam is seen as dependable and unchanging. Every aspect of Muslim behavior is guided by the Koran, the holy book of Islam. For example, the Koran dictates what kind of art and decoration are allowed; in Islam, it is forbidden to portray anything from nature in art. The rules regarding the way men and women relate to one another are also drawn from the Koran.

Festival spectators pull back to make room for the horsemen, who ride past at great speed.

The First Lady's Concert and Competition

Nike and many other schoolchildren in Lagos have been looking forward to a special concert for the Nigerian Children's Trust Fund. Nigeria's first lady, the wife of the president, has organized and is the guest of honor at this event. The concert is for the benefit of children who are in special need of welfare and social services, especially children with disabilities.

The concert also includes a children's competition in art, singing, dancing, poetry, and drama. Winners from each of Nigeria's 30 states have come to Lagos to represent their state. Dressed in their traditional costumes, the children display their talents as they compete. Competitions are also held for sculpture, painting, and pottery.

Nike was supposed to go to the First Lady's Concert with her schoolmates, but their bus wasn't available. Instead, she went with her nephew to see the winning artwork.

Uloma Agbugba, the first prize winner, is an 11-year-old girl from Imo State. She won for her sculpture of a crocodile, which she made from newspapers, starch, and water.

Trying to get donations from concert spectators, the first lady speaks movingly about the plight of Nigerian children living with disabilities, in poverty, or orphaned.

Dancers in matching costumes wait to perform.

These two young girls are competing in a singing and dancing contest.

First prize winner Uloma Agbugba stands in front of a colorful poster announcing the First Lady's Concert and Competition.

Nike, An Athlete and Budding Politician

Nike is great at sports. Last year, she won first prize in a running contest that brought together students from many private schools. She is house captain, or leader, of her running team at St. Saviour's School.

In a race at the International School on Victoria Island in Lagos one Saturday morning, Nike competed for St. Saviour's School against the International School and the French school. Although she loves to compete and had hoped to run in several longer races, Nike ran only in the 100 meters contest because she had a cold.

A very determined girl, Nike tries as hard as she can, no matter what activity she's doing. Although she's only ten years old, she has an idea of what she wants to be when she grows up — a politician. This kind of work requires one to know how to get along with different people and how to speak different languages. Nike is already very good at both those things. She's eager to do whatever needs to be done to make her life, and her country, better.

Dotun, Nike's older brother, whispers a few encouraging words in her ear.

After the race, the girls stretch out on a bench.

Nike rests on the grass after a hard race.

47

FOR YOUR INFORMATION: Nigeria

Official Name: Federal Republic of Nigeria

Capital: Lagos and Abuja

History

The First Inhabitants: Prehistory

The region now known as Nigeria was inhabited at least 10,000 years ago by tribes that lived in the savannas and forests along the Niger River. These groups lived for thousands of years by hunting wildlife and gathering wild foods. By about 1000 BC, farmers had begun growing crops near the forests.

By 500 BC, the Nok people had built a flourishing civilization. They lived along the fertile banks where two great rivers, the Niger and the Benue, meet. They knew the secret of smelting iron more than 2,000 years ago and left behind iron tools, stone axes and ornaments, and many terra-cotta figures. By about AD 200, their civilization had died out.

After skillfully guiding logs cut in Nigeria's forests down the Niger River, loggers lash the timbers together into rafts. This lumber will eventually be sold to factories.

The Yoruba, Ibo, and Ijaw Peoples

The great variety of people who live in Nigeria today have roots that go back more than 1,000 years. For example, for as long as people have told stories about their history, the Yoruba people and their kingdoms have dominated the Niger's west bank. The Yoruba may have migrated into Nigeria from Egypt and settled into the southern coastal region between the 11th and 14th centuries. Ruled by chieftains, they lived in great cities surrounded by square walls built of baked mud. Among these early kingdoms were the cities of Ife, Oyo, and Benin. The Yoruba knew how to cast brass and bronze figures and used these objects to trade with people from North Africa and later, from Europe.

The Yoruba also traded in slaves who were taken from weaker tribes that had been conquered in war. Conquered tribes also gave some slaves to chiefs as payment of taxes. Ife was the center of the slave trade with the countries to the north. By the 15th century, the riches of this trade supported Benin's 100,000 people. It became the center of the area known as Yorubaland. Oyo grew so large that it began to overlap areas controlled by other people, and in time, it was destroyed.

On the east bank of the Niger River lived the Ibo and Ijaw peoples. Unlike the Yoruba, they lived in small villages and were not ruled by chiefs. But they, too, were active in the slave trade and used their money to buy land, an important measure of wealth. Land ownership was an unusual concept in Africa at this time, setting the Ibo apart from other tribes.

The Bornu, Hausa, and Fulani Peoples

Far to the north lived the Bornu and the Hausa. The Bornu settled first in the region of Lake Chad in the northeast. Islamic preachers began to travel into this area from farther north and slowly converted the local people to their religion. By AD 1000, the Bornu kingdom had become a center of Islamic culture and learning. They, too, took part in the slave trade.

Around AD 1000, the Hausa began to move into the northern area from the Sudan, peacefully absorbing people from many cultures as they traveled. The term "Hausa" refers to the language, not to a culture. The absorbed people learned to speak Hausa, now one of the most widely spoken languages in the north. The Hausa also lived in great walled cities with as many as 50,000 people. Kano, one of the seven Hausa city-states founded in the north before 1100, was a great center of Islamic learning with cultural and economic ties to Islamic centers far away in North Africa. Unlike the Ibo, the Hausa measured wealth in cattle, not land.

The Fulani began migrating into Hausaland in the 13th century, moving southward to escape the drying up of the Sahara. They were known as a religious and educated people.

Slavery and a *Jihad*

In 1472, the Portuguese, who were exploring the entire West African coast, were the first Europeans to land in Nigeria. Although they did not establish any settlements, their skills as navigators made it possible for slaves to be transported across the ocean. Previously, slaves were only traded locally. Slaves who were sent away by ship never saw their homelands again.

In 1486, a Portuguese explorer named John Affonso d'Aveiro reached Benin City. This was the start of a long trading relationship with the people of Benin. The Portuguese traded firearms for slaves and for peppers, an important spice.

In the north, the influence of Islam continued to shape the way people thought and lived their lives. During the reign of Idris Alooma from 1571 to 1603, the laws of the Islamic religion, known as Sharia, were put into effect, taking the place of the customary laws. This became the basis for the differences between northern and southern Nigeria, differences that have divided the nation ever since.

The city of Oyo continued to expand its territory. By the 18th century, it had reached far to the west and north and was beginning to spill over onto the coastal ports, where it came into conflict with the Fulani.

In the early 19th century, this conflict led to a *jihad* — a war fought to defend and promote the Islamic religion. The "settled" Fulani, who lived in towns and cities, overran the land and divided it up among their emirs. They were helped by the people known as the "cattle" Fulani, who lived a nomadic life with an economy based entirely on their cattle. These two groups established the Fulani as the ruling tribe in the region.

Great Britain Dominates Nigeria

Beginning in the 1700s and continuing for the next 150 years, Great Britain used slave labor from Africa for its plantations. After Britain outlawed slavery at home in 1807, it conquered and then annexed the port city of Lagos in 1861 to put an end to the slave trade in Nigeria and other countries.

By 1878, the United Africa Company, a British company, was trading along the Niger River. The traders, who were moving farther into the interior, requested Britain's protection. So in 1885, the Niger River Delta was established as a British protectorate. Later that year, the European powers met and divided up Africa among the European countries. They agreed that Great Britain could claim Nigeria, but the Africans were never asked what they thought about this agreement. In 1886, the United Africa Company became known as the Royal Niger Company and actually governed the territory under a charter from Britain.

In 1900, Britain put northern Nigeria under the control of the British Colonial Office. The Fulani had their own system of chiefs, and the British decided to leave that system alone and govern by giving laws to the local officials. The Yoruba, in the west, also had a strong system of chiefs. In other areas, such as the southeast where the Ibos lived and where there was no system of chiefs, the British took direct control. The Ibos helped the British in the day-to-day running of the government through their jobs in the civil service.

In addition, Christian missionaries had set up schools to educate the people in the south. Because the north was under Islamic rule, the missionaries were not permitted to go there. The differences between northern and southern Nigeria continued to grow.

In 1922, a new British constitution left the north as it was but divided the south into eastern and western regions. For the first time, some representatives were elected by Nigerians. This was the beginning of the growth of nationalism in Nigeria, a sense that all the different tribes belonged to one country.

Independence and Experiments in Government

A series of new forms of government was tried over the years leading up to independence in 1960. Each new form was an attempt to bring the three areas of the country — the north, the southeast, and the southwest — under one form of government. Pressure on the British was constant as each area of the country demanded its own share of representation. By 1957, each of the three regions of the country had become self-governing.

The Nigerians kept demanding more control over their own lives, until finally the British granted Nigeria its independence on October 1, 1960, as a federation of three regions — northern, western, and eastern. Nigeria became a parliamentary republic within the British Commonwealth of Nations.

The nation of Nigeria that was born in 1960 was a loose federation with more than 250 ethnic and linguistic groups. The seeds for future conflict were present from the moment the nation gained its independence because of the different political and ethnic factions. The nation struggled to find a workable system, trying out various new ways to divide up the land. In 1963, Nigeria proclaimed itself a federal republic with a new constitution and added a fourth region — the midwest. In 1966, two military coups shook the country, and Nigeria saw the massacre of thousands of Ibos in the north. In May 1967, the country was reorganized into 12 states. And also in 1967, a civil war began that nearly tore the country apart.

The Biafra War

On May 30, 1967, Odumegwu Emeka Ojukwu, the leader of the eastern region, declared his part of the country, where the Ibos lived, to be a separate nation called Biafra. The Ibos were among the most skilled and educated people in Nigeria, working as technicians, clerks, and civil servants. Many returned to the region to take part in the fighting. The eastern region is an oil-producing area, and the Nigerians were determined to keep it.

A 30-month-long civil war followed. Hundreds of thousands of people were killed. Many more, most of them children, died from starvation because the Nigerian government stopped food shipments to the eastern region from other countries. The war finally ended in January of 1970, when the enormous Nigerian army defeated the Biafran rebels. An estimated one to two million people had died. Many were killed, while others died of hunger and disease.

Dizzying Changes

Lieutenant Colonel Yakubu Gowon had taken control of the government during the war, fighting against Colonel Ojukwu. In 1975, Gowon was overthrown by the army, beginning a dizzying series of coups, assassinations, and army takeovers. The new chief of staff, Army Brigadier Muritala Rufai Mohammed, became the new chief of state and announced a return to civilian rule by 1979. One year later, he was assassinated. A new leader, General Olusegun Obasanjo, took over. In 1977, he created seven new states, thus bringing the total number of states to 19. A new capital was to be built later in the Federal Capital Territory.

A new constitution was published in 1978, and the country returned to civilian rule in 1979 when Alhaji Shehu Shagari was elected president. While this election ended 12 years of military rule, the new democratic and civilian government stayed in power for only four years. On December 31, 1983, the military, under Major General Mohammed Buhari, overthrew the government. General Buhari was himself overthrown on August 27, 1985, in a coup led by Major General Ibrahim Badamasi Babangida, who proclaimed himself president and continued to rule into the 1990s. Although he is considered one of the best rulers of Nigeria, Babangida has never been elected president. But he has promised that democratic elections for the presidency of Nigeria will be held in late 1992.

Government

Since the military coup of 1983, the 1979 constitution has been suspended, and the Armed Forces Ruling Council (AFRC) currently governs the country. President Babangida is chairman of the AFRC, head of state, and chief of the armed forces.

Men paddle a dugout canoe along a river.

A new constitution similar to the 1979 one is expected to go into effect on October 1, 1992. Under this constitution, there are to be three independent branches of government: executive, legislative, and judicial. Voters are to choose a president and elect members to fill the Senate and the House of Representatives of the National Assembly. They are also to elect governors for each of the states as well as representatives for the state assemblies. The number of states, now 30, has increased several times since independence.

Although reforms put into effect during Buhari's term from 1983 to 1985 were meant to lessen corruption, they haven't been very successful. For example, new construction projects are always delayed because so many people involved in the projects steal the money and the materials before they reach building sites. In addition, the federal government keeps more than half of the taxes collected, leaving just 31.5% of the money for the states and only 10% for local governments. A great deal of these funds winds up in the hands of individuals who spend them on themselves, not on making things better for Nigeria and its citizens. Under military rule, some basic human rights are denied; for example, people can be detained for indefinite periods without trial.

In late 1990, two political parties — the Social Democratic Party and the National Republican Convention — were established. These are the only two political parties to receive financial aid and administrative support from the government and to enter the 1992 legislative elections.

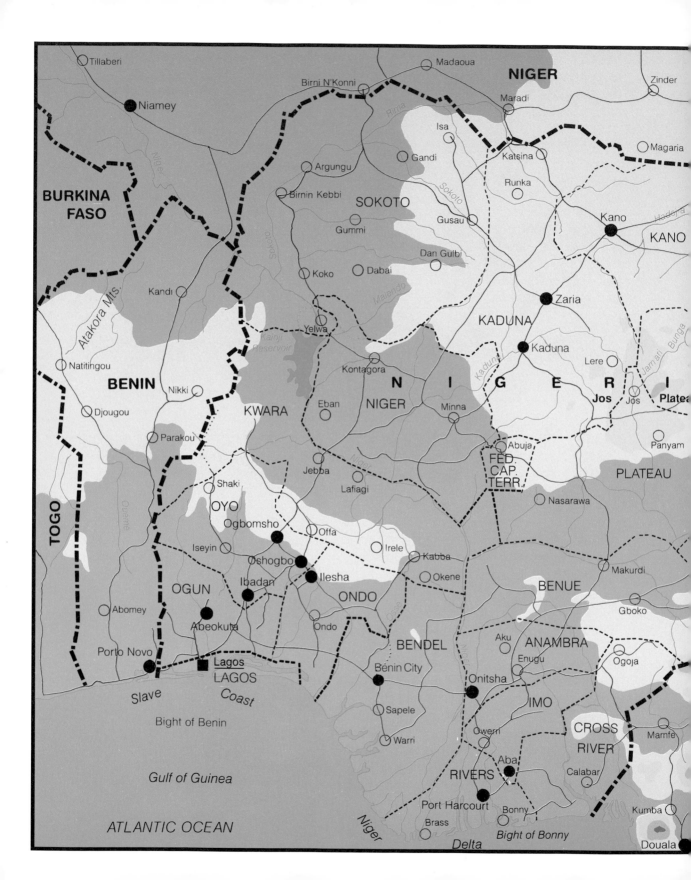

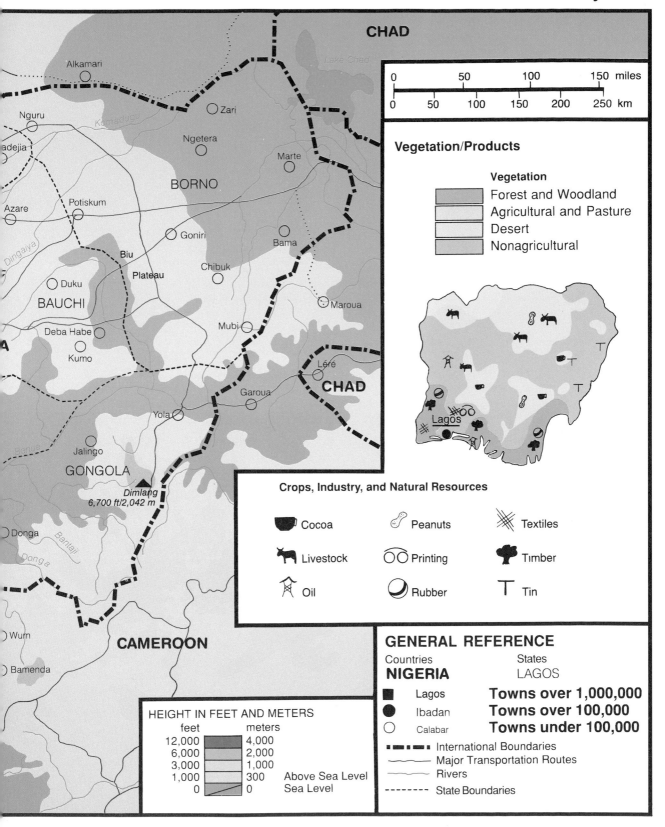

NIGERIA – Political and Physical

CHAD

Lake Chad

Alkamari

Zari

Nguru

Komadugu

Ngetera

adejia

Marte

BORNO

Azare

Potiskum

Goniri

Bama

Dingaiya

Biu

Plateau

Chibuk

Duku

Maroua

BAUCHI

Mubi

Deba Habe

Kumo

Lére

Garoua

CHAD

Yola

Jalingo

GONGOLA

▲ Dimlang
6,700 ft/2,042 m

Donga

Benue

Bantaji

Donga

Wum

CAMEROON

Bamenda

Vegetation/Products

Vegetation

Forest and Woodland
Agricultural and Pasture
Desert
Nonagricultural

Lagos

| 0 | 50 | 100 | 150 miles |
| 0 | 50 | 100 | 150 | 200 | 250 km |

Crops, Industry, and Natural Resources

Cocoa   Peanuts   Textiles

Livestock   Printing   Timber

Oil   Rubber   Tin

GENERAL REFERENCE

| Countries | States |
| **NIGERIA** | LAGOS |

■ Lagos — **Towns over 1,000,000**

● Ibadan — **Towns over 100,000**

○ Calabar — **Towns under 100,000**

▬ International Boundaries
── Major Transportation Routes
── Rivers
------ State Boundaries

HEIGHT IN FEET AND METERS

feet	meters
12,000	4,000
6,000	2,000
3,000	1,000
1,000	300
0	0

Above Sea Level
Sea Level

Land and Climate

Nigeria is located along the Gulf of Guinea on the southern coast of western Africa. It shares borders with Benin, Niger, Chad, and Cameroon. Nigeria covers an area of 356,700 square miles (924,630 sq km) — slightly less than the size of British Columbia but more than twice the size of California. Two major rivers flow through Nigeria — the Niger, from which the country got its name, and the Benue.

The climate in the southern part of the country is hot and humid. A wide belt of swamps and mangrove trees thrives along the coast. The coastal area is quite flat, often merging with the sea. Inland, the land rises up to 4,360 feet (1,320 m) along the Jos Plateau. Northward, the land gives way to a stretch of dense jungle, where trees grow 200 feet (61 m) tall. As much as 150 inches (381 cm) of rain falls here during the year, making this area damp, green, and full of vegetation and wildlife.

Well to the north, the climate becomes less humid, finally reaching near-desert conditions in the extreme north where Nigeria meets the Sahara. From the earliest time in Nigeria's history, northern peoples began moving south because their lands were growing drier and less productive. This land between the Sahara and the more fertile lands to the south is called the Sahel.

There are two seasons in Nigeria: rainy and dry. It begins raining infrequently in April, but by July, it is raining every day. This lasts a total of six months, until October. The dry season follows for another six months. During the dry season, a hot trade wind called the Harmattan blows over the land from the desert for more than three months. When the wind isn't blowing, the temperature drops to its lowest point of the year. The average temperature in the south is about 80°F (27°C). In the north, daily temperatures may rise above 100°F (38°C) but drop by more than 40°F (23°C) at night.

Agriculture, Industry, and Natural Resources

Nigeria's most important natural resource is oil. It is one of the major oil producing countries in the world. Much of the oil comes from the area around Port Harcourt on the Gulf of Guinea. Oil is an unpredictable source of income since its price varies in reaction to world events. For example, during the 1991 war in the Persian Gulf, the price of oil doubled, only to fall again a few months later.

Before the discovery of oil, Nigeria's major export was cocoa, which is used in making chocolate. Nigeria also exports some rubber, timber, and tin, but oil accounts for over 95% of its foreign income. Other agricultural products include peanuts, cotton, grains, fish, and cattle. Cattle raising is limited to the north, which is free of tsetse flies. These tiny insects carry diseases like sleeping sickness that kill cattle.

Peoples and Languages

An estimated 250 different ethnic groups live in Nigeria, speaking at least that many distinctly different languages. It is Africa's most ethnically diverse country. Although there is no official count of Nigeria's population, the estimate as of 1990 was 119,800,000. With the largest population of any African country, Nigeria accounts for about one-quarter of all the people in Africa and the greatest number of people living in cities.

The number of people in each region is a matter of great conflict within Nigeria, since each region wants to have more representatives in government. Census figures are normally used to decide how to distribute political power and government revenues. The government, centered in the south, generally ignores census figures if they show the north is more populous than the south. The results of the 1973 census were so unsatisfactory to the government that it refused to allow them to be published, and there hasn't been an official census since. Meanwhile, the economic and political problems and the population continue to grow.

Four of Nigeria's major ethnic groups are the Hausa, Fulani, Yoruba, and Ibo. The Fulani and Hausa are the major Islamic peoples while the Ibo and the Yoruba are the major Christian groups. The Hausa-speaking people live in a wide area spread over the northwest. Nigerians from different cultures who live in this area also speak Hausa, in part because it is a relatively easy language to learn. The Fulani also live in northern Nigeria, but their culture stretches to neighboring countries. Many Fulani still follow a nomadic life, moving with their cattle to new grazing areas. Others have settled in towns and have become active in promoting and maintaining the importance of Islam in daily life.

The Yoruba inhabit a wide area of southwestern Nigeria as well as the neighboring countries of Benin, Togo, and Ghana. Before Christianity was introduced, their culture was centered on the religious belief that spirits caused everyday problems. If you could ease those spirits, then your daily life would be happier. The Ibo live in southeastern Nigeria and are the third largest ethnic group in Nigeria. Through the centuries, they have lived in small family groups without a system of chiefs. They have always appreciated and rewarded individual achievements.

These larger tribal groupings are only part of the picture of life in Nigeria. The large number of tribes, each with its own language and customs, helps keep people in the rural areas in great isolation, even though they may live only a few miles apart.

English is Nigeria's official language and the language of instruction in school from the fourth grade up. In the north, Hausa often replaces English as the most commonly used language. Other major languages are Fulani, Yoruba, and Ibo.

Education

Nigeria's educational system is compulsory and free for the first six years of primary school. After that, children who pass the "school-leavers" examination may go on to secondary school. The emphasis in primary school is on reading and arithmetic with an overall goal of preparing students to be good citizens. Though almost half the population of Nigeria is 15 years old or younger, for a number of reasons only about 12 million students are in primary school. Schooling is not easily available in rural areas; government funding is insufficient; children often have too much work to do at home to attend school; and a very low level of teaching discourages attendance. In Muslim northern Nigeria, schooling is limited to little beyond learning to read holy texts. Public education at the secondary level is available in some of the southwestern states. There are about 25 universities in Nigeria. About one-third of the people of Nigeria are able to read and write.

Art

The carvings of the Yoruba are known throughout the world, and many of the ancient pieces from their city of Ife have survived in excellent condition. The Yoruba worked mostly in brass, which they cast, and in terra-cotta as well as in stone. When we think of typical African sculpture, especially the faces with large oval eyes and full lips, we are really seeing Yoruba art.

The rich cultural life of Benin in southern Nigeria may be seen in its intricate bronze sculptures. They are so carefully made that you can see how people looked and dressed hundreds of years ago. Some are made in the form of animals that reveal the kinds of creatures that were common in the area then: leopards, crocodiles, snakes, birds, and fish.

Nigeria has also given birth to many great writers, such as the poet, playwright, and novelist Wole Soyinka, who won a Nobel Prize. Noted writer

Chinua Achebe captured the essence of life in colonial-era Nigeria in his book *Things Fall Apart.*

Religion

Today, it is estimated that 47% of the people follow the Islamic religion, while 34% are Christians. About 18% are animist, followers of traditional religions who believe that the spirit of God may be felt in any living thing.

The Islamic religion in northern Nigeria arrived in the state of Bornu from farther north and was spread by contact with the Arabs. But it was not until the arrival of the British in the mid-19th century that substantial numbers of Christian missionaries came in and began claiming large numbers of converts. Their activities were restricted to the south so as not to offend the leaders in the north. The result: a north-south split in religion that continues to this day.

Sports and Recreation

Nigeria was the first black African nation to participate in the Olympics. In 1984, Nigeria won a bronze medal in a relay race in the Los Angeles games. As in much of Africa, its people are mad about soccer, and Nigeria fields a team in the World Cup games. In the cities, television brings such sports into the homes, creating a huge number of devoted fans. Wrestling and cricket are also popular.

Currency

Nigeria's unit of currency is called the *naira,* which is divided into 100 *kobo.* Practically speaking, only naira notes are in circulation. There are one-, five-, ten-, and 20-naira notes. A 50-kobo note exists but is rarely seen. A one-naira coin is going to be minted because the one-naira bills wear out so quickly. Important figures in Nigeria's history are portrayed on the bills. In 1992, the naira was worth about ten cents.

A fisherman casts his nets, which look like butterfly wings.

Lagos

The most crowded city in Nigeria is the capital, Lagos. About seven to ten million people are crowded into the city center and the surrounding areas. People sometimes spend an entire day in a traffic jam here, so the street vendors do a lively business. To reduce congestion, only half the licensed cars are allowed to travel on each weekday. If people are caught driving on the wrong day, they are fined heavily.

To improve the environment in Lagos, the government has ordered everyone to spend three hours once a month at some clean-up task. During this time, no one may be in any kind of vehicle, not in an airplane or even on a bicycle. The military is always around to be sure these rules are followed.

In Lagos, electricity is undependable. There are often blackouts, even in the best neighborhoods. The phone system is so unpredictable that many business people employ messengers to deliver information.

For all these reasons, a more centrally located capital has been planned at Abuja in the Federal Capital Territory. Building this capital has been underway for about 20 years and is expected to continue into the next century.

Nigerians in North America

Nigerians who come to the United States often settle in cities with climates like those they knew at home, cities such as Houston, Atlanta, Los Angeles, and Washington, DC. Canada also has large communities of Nigerians in Toronto, Vancouver, and Montreal. Many of these people came during the 1960s and 1970s to study and stayed. More recently, Nigerians have come to North America to escape the poor economic conditions in Nigeria. There are thought to be about 20,000 Nigerians currently studying in the United States and several hundred thousand Nigerians living there. Many come on tourist visas and then decide not to go home.

More Books about Nigeria

A Family in Nigeria. Barker (Lerner)
The Moonlight Bride. Emecheta (George Braziller)
Nigeria in Pictures. Department of Geography (Lerner)
The Wrestling Match. Emecheta (George Braziller)

Glossary of Important Terms

cassava ....plant with a large starchy root used as a staple food and in tapioca.
emirs ....tribal chiefs.
nationalism ....a feeling of pride in one's country that unites people from different cultures.
plantain ....a fruit similar to a banana.
protectorate ......a country under the protection and partial control of another county.
terra-cotta ....a clay that is formed in a mold and then fired in a kiln.

Glossary of Useful Yoruba Terms

baba (BAH-bah) ....father
ile-iwe (ee-LEH-ee-WEH) ....school
iya (ee-YAH)......................................mother
oluko (oh-loo-KOO) ....teacher
omo (aw-mah)...................................boy or child
ore (aw-REH) ....friend
iyawo (ee-AH-woe) ....girl

Things to Do — Research Projects and Activities

Nigeria's frequent changes in government, from democratic to military and back again, make it a fascinating country. With its big population and its oil wealth, Nigeria could be a leader among African nations. What is its role in the Organization for African Unity? To find out about changes in Nigeria's leadership and other matters of current interest in recent newspaper and magazine articles, look up *Nigeria* in these two publications:

Readers' Guide to Periodical Literature
Children's Magazine Guide

1. The art created in Nigeria is probably the best known art from Africa. Look up Nigerian art in your library, using the names of the different cultures, such as Hausa, Yoruba, Benin, and Ibo. See if there is an exhibit in your local museum. Try to create objects or drawings similar to those you find.

2. Nigeria is a country with three distinct regions. Compare these regions by studying the cultures of the Hausa, the Yoruba, and the Ibo. Write a report on the differences in religion and systems of chiefs.

3. Many slave ships started out from Africa at the port of Lagos. Try to find out how many people were taken as slaves from Africa and to which countries they were taken.

4. Nigeria has a wide variety of climates. What kind of homes do you think people should live in if they live in the north of Nigeria, where it's very hot and dry, and in the south, where it's very rainy. Draw pictures of these homes.

5. If you would like to have a Nigerian pen pal, write to these groups:

International Pen Friends
P.O. Box 290065
Brooklyn, NY 11229

Worldwide Pen Friends
P.O. Box 39097
Downey, CA 90241

Be sure to tell them what country you want your pen pal to be from and your full name, address, and age.

Index